Her Inspiration

Her Inspiration

Secrets to Help You
Work Smart, Be Successful, and Have Fun

Mina Parker ⋯ foreword by BJ Gallagher

Conari Press

First published in 2008 by Conari Press,
an imprint of Red Wheel/Weiser, LLC
With offices at:
500 Third Street, Suite 230
San Francisco, CA 94107
www.redwheelweiser.com

ISBN-10: 1-57324-324-8
ISBN-13: 978-1-57324-324-7
Library of Congress Cataloging-in-Publication Data is available upon request

Cover and text design by Kristine Brogno.
Typeset in Emmascript, Garamond, and Neutra.
Cover illustration © 2008 Karn Knutson, *greenfacedgirl.com*.

Printed in Canada
FR
10 9 8 7 6 5 4 3 2 1

The paper used in this publication meets the minimum requirements of the American
National Standard for Information Sciences—Permanence of Paper for Printed Library
Materials Z39.48-1992 (R1997).

Contents

Foreword by BJ Gallagher   6

Be Inspired: Secrets of Highly Successful Women   8

Get Organized: Tips and Time-savers   11

Chill: Give Yourself a Break   33

Create Your Style: Fashion Sense and Common Sense   55

Gather Your Group: Friends, Mentors, and Motivators   81

Indulge Yourself: Little Rewards Lead to Big Accomplishments   103

Live Well: Living Your Life to the Hilt   123

Be Bold: How to Make Your Ideas Count   149

Work Smart: Loving Your Job and Being the Best You Can Be!   173

Achieve: Women Can Do Anything!   197

Foreword

Wisdom, thy name is Woman.

The volume you hold in your hands is a wonderful compilation of quips and quotes by inspiring women. They are mothers, sisters, daughters, aunts, grandmas, girlfriends, neighbors, classmates, and coworkers.

Some are famous—others not. But they all have uttered words that can teach, console, lift us up out of our doldrums, and share words of wisdom for our journey through Life, and this is a book to turn to again and again for advice, support, encouragement, empathy, and understanding.

As you'll see, wisdom isn't limited to those of fame and fortune. Some of the wisest words I've ever heard came from the lips of ordinary women of extraordinary insight, like Suzanne Schultz, a researcher at the University of Delaware who once said, "The greatest gift you can give someone is the gift of the interested listener." Or my dear friend Karen Cutts, who likes to say, "Don't let what you can't do stop you from what you can do." My female friends and colleagues may come and go, but their wise words stay with me forever.

That's not to say that famous women aren't great sources of inspiration, too, because they are. For sure. And this book offers you the gift of their words as well.

Mina Parker's collection, *Her Inspiration*, is a veritable treasure chest of pearls of wisdom and wit from women. Words to live by—words to love by—words to laugh by. Words of wisdom from women who fan the flame of hope that each of us can design the kind of life we want to live—we don't have to buy into anyone else's definition of success, happiness, or fulfillment.

These are pearls of great worth. Try them on—see how they feel—choose the pearls that best suit you and the kind of life you aspire to. Keep them close to your heart. Every woman needs a good string of pearls...pearls of wisdom, that is.

BJ Gallagher, author of *Everything I Need to Know I Learned from Other Women, Friends Are Everything,* and *Women's Work Is Never Done*

Be Inspired

SECRETS *of* HIGHLY SUCCESSFUL WOMEN

Women inspire me. It's as simple as that. All I have to do is look around. There are the women who run the restaurant on the corner—the place where everybody feels comfortable and taken care of. There are mothers pushing strollers, and mothers crunching numbers. There are women healing the sick. Gals cracking us up. Ladies penning the novels and singing the songs that change our lives. Chicks fixing the plumbing. Girls setting world records. Politicians challenging the status quo from within the system, and activists battering it from the outside. There are women at the pinnacle of their fields in every corner of the world, and women finding satisfaction in their own successes, small and large. What's their secret? (Well, I'll give you a hint…there's more than one.)

What kind of success are you working toward? Maybe you don't know yet—or thought you did but aren't sure. Or maybe you're on the right track but need a kick in the pants.

In our own lives, success can feel elusive. We can get bogged down comparing ourselves to others, or whining about what we lack. The women in this book have secrets to share, to shout to the rafters even. Their wise words will push your buttons, open your eyes, and rev up your engine.

This book is a reminder that you have what it takes to make it to the top. And the best part is, you get to decide where the top is and you get to chart the path to reach it. This book is here for you—it's full of quotes and thoughts from hundreds of women to encourage, motivate, and support you as you make your way. Famous and infamous, wise and wisecracking, haughty and humble. Some are names you will know well, others are everyday gals like you and me with something important to add.

I read somewhere that we're all descended from three ancestral mothers. How amazing is that? A woman brought each and every one of us into this world, and when we look in the mirror we can see traces of our mothers, grandmothers, even great-grandmothers. And their gifts go way beyond skin deep. Every woman in the world is a member of this family—and you can call on their words and their life stories to inspire you at every turn. So keep this book close to you as you get organized, vamp up your personal style, and figure out how to work smarter. Sit back and let this book help you remember the importance of relaxing and indulging yourself (with girlfriends whenever possible). And don't ever forget to go after your dreams with every ounce of yourself, because after all—women can do anything!

One

Get Organized
TIPS and TIME-SAVERS

If managing your life feels like a war, then half of every battle is getting things in order. For me it's no fun at all. I have this nagging feeling that I have two lives going on simultaneously: the fun stuff and the rest of it. For example, I love to cook but despise washing dishes. I love the feeling of paying off the monthly bills, but often can't get myself together to do it until a week past the deadline, and then I feel miserable about the cumulative effect on my credit score. And any upheaval—a move, an emergency, or just getting a bad head cold—throws me for a loop. *How did I let this go?!* I ask myself, crazed. *Why is my house filled with paper?!* (One in every five pieces is really important, I swear.)

Well, it's time for a detox, a deep cleansing, spring cleaning. Doing your taxes. Clearing and sorting your wardrobe. Getting rid of the magazines you've been unwittingly storing since college. What a wonderful release. Now, those are the big projects, and don't worry yourself into trying to do them all at once. Just pick a project each month and do it a little at a time or set aside a whole weekend to blast through, whatever suits your style.

And for the rest of the month take aim at the little, repetitive, everyday stuff. Work hard to make it a habit to sort your mail right away, clean out your pockets and purse every day, and dream up new ways to multitask effectively. Train yourself to make a difference in tiny ways all day long, and soon you'll forget it's an annoyance because when it all adds up, you're way ahead of the game. If you can coax yourself into making the art of organization second nature, I promise it will serve you forever.

Find Your Focus

Words are a lens to focus one's mind.

AYN RAND

Sometimes I still lose my head, even though it
is attached to my body. But if I've left myself
a note, I can usually find it again.

MARLO THOMAS

Detail is electric.

BONNI GOLDBERG

To know where you can find a thing
is the chief part of learning.

UNKNOWN

Only when your consciousness is totally focused
on the moment you are in can you receive whatever
gift, lesson, or delight that moment has to offer.

BARBARA DE ANGELIS

On clutter: chaos begets chaos in our homes,
and in our minds.

CAROL WISEMAN

A place for everything, and everything in its place.

ISABELLA MARY BEETON

Just before bedtime prayers, evaluate each day.
Make plans for tomorrow that will move you
toward your long-range goal.

FLORENCE S. JACOBSEN

You may not be able to foresee what the universe
has planned for you, but that doesn't mean
your own plans should be unpredictable.

SANDRA OLIVER

Most of what you obtain in life will be because of your
discipline. Discipline is perhaps more important than ability.

CHRISTINE DARDEN

Never walk into or out of a meeting without a clear agenda.

MARY JANE RYAN

Many a woman has a "to do list" that resembles
the phone book! Don't over do your "to do" list.
Keep it reasonable and keep it doable.

LESLIE ROSSMAN

I want minimum information given
with maximum politeness.

JACKIE KENNEDY

Out your problem on a piece of paper, stick the paper
in a drawer and close it. Do not allow yourself to
look at or think about the list until the end of the week.
By then, you may will look at your problems
differently and will have solutions.

MICHELLE STRONG

I don't wait for moods. You accomplish
nothing if you do that. Your mind must know
it has got to get down to work.

PEARL S. BUCK

Plan and Prepare

Look twice before you leap.

CHARLOTTE BRONTË

The very best impromptu speeches are
the ones written well in advance.

RUTH GORDON

What I've learned from fairy tales:
Invest in some good string rather than mere breadcrumbs.
That way, you can always find the path back
to the gingerbread house.

WENDY ST. CHARLES

Failing to plan is planning to fail.

EFFIE JONES

If one asks for success and prepares for failure,
she will get the situation she has prepared for.

FLORENCE SCOVEL SHINN

Don't agonize. Organize.

FLORYNCE KENNEDY

Plans are necessary to life and achievement
in any sphere. But they should never
overcome our powers of flexibility.

DIXIE MARTIN

Lack of confidence is born from a lack of preparation.

SHANNON WILBURN

Luck is a matter of preparation meeting opportunity.

OPRAH WINFREY

You had better live your best and act your best and think your best today; for today is the sure preparation for tomorrow and all the other tomorrows that follow.

HARRIET MARTINEAU

Winning is the science of being totally prepared.

GRACIE ALLEN

Preparation, I have often said,
is rightly two-thirds of any venture.

AMELIA EARHART

Dream On!

Fantasies are more than substitutes for unpleasant reality;
they are also dress rehearsals, plans. All acts performed
in the world begin in the imagination.

BARBARA GRIZZUTI HARRISON

What the world really needs is more love and less paperwork.

PEARL BAILEY

If we would only give, just once, the same amount of reflection
to what we want to get out of life that we give to the question
of what to do with a two weeks' vacation, we would be
startled at the aimless procession of our busy days.

DOROTHY CANFIELD FISHER

I want to so order my life that its impression, its impact, might always be positive and spiritually constructive.

DOROTHY BROWN

For the happiest life, days should be rigorously planned, nights left open to chance.

MIGNON McLAUGHLIN

To stay ahead, you must have your next idea waiting in the wings.

ROSABETH MOSS KANTER

All the flowers of all the tomorrows are in the seeds of today.

PROVERB

Make big plans; aim high in hope and work,

remembering that a noble and logical plan never dies,

but long after we are gone will be a living thing.

LITA BANE

It's never too late—in fiction or in life—to revise.

NANCY THAYER

Take Your Life in Your Own Hands

It's true that life's gifts come with responsibilities. When I don't feel like cleaning up my desk or my car or my house or my general existence, I try to remember the people who would be desperate to have all the things I take for granted.

RACHEL CLARKSON

You take your life in your own hands, and what happens?
A terrible thing: no one to blame.

ERICA JONG

Make decisions in a timely fashion—
rarely does waiting improve the quality of the decision.

ODETTE POLLAR

This is a wonderful world for women. The richness, the hope, the promise of life today...are exciting beyond belief. Nonetheless, we need stout hearts and strong characters; we need knowledge and training; we need organized effort to meet the future.

BELLE S. SPAFFORD

When planning for a year, plant corn.
When planning for a decade, plant trees.
When planning for life, train and educate people.

PROVERB

I don't know that there are any
shortcuts to doing a good job.

SANDRA DAY O'CONNOR

I was taught the way of progress is neither swift nor easy.

MARIE CURIE

Some Helpful How-To's

I must govern the clock, not be governed by it.

GOLDA MEIR

If only everything were as easily organized as, say, my shoe
collection. And even that can sometimes be a losing battle.

SASHA MORROW

There are so many options, so much to do, so many
demands on women. There is no point in taking one hour
to do a ten-minute task, nor should we slap together
an hour-worthy project in ten minutes.

ELAINE CANNON

Arrange whatever pieces come your way.

VIRGINIA WOOLF

A team is more than a collection of people.

It is a process of give and take.

BARBARA GLACEL

Effective teamwork is all about making a good, well-balanced

salad, not whipping individuals into a single batch of V8.

SANDRA RICHARDSON

Take just a few minutes each day to sort through any

miscellaneous papers on your desk at home or the office,

rather than letting unorganized piles multiply and grow.

GLADYS MORISSON

To achieve your dreams, remember your ABC's:

Avoid negative sources, people, places, things, and habits.

Believe in yourself.

Consider things from every angle.

WANDA HOPE CARTER

Keep things as simple as possible...

nobody wants to reorganize their system of organization!

CASSIE LAWRENCE

If a problem has no solution,

it's not a problem, just a fact.

BJ GALLAGHER

There are two ways of meeting difficulties.
You alter the difficulties or you alter yourself to meet them.

PHYLLIS BOTTOMED

Adopt the highly effective SAW inbox system:
Stat (as in a hospital Emergency Room) means "do it now!"
and is for urgent tasks with a deadline of today.
A stands for "as soon as possible" and goes on your "to-do list"
with doable deadlines. W stands for "whenever" and is
only for "ideas" and wishes for the future.

ROBERTA LEFFLER

I always say don't make plans, make options.

JENNIFER ANISTON

Get a 3-ring binder with pocketed dividers for receipts
and user-manuals, and organize by need such as
"birthdays," "utility bills," "credit cards and reports,"
"computer info," and most importantly, "taxes!"

NINA LESOWITZ

One way to keep control over the paper in your life is to
get it back in circulation—do you have a stack of magazines
that you are almost "done" with? Take a few moments to go
through them and then pass them on to friends, a library,
a school, a hospital, or a charity thrift shop. I have a
magazine "trade" system set up with some girlfriends!

LILLIAN CRIST

The most successful people in the world break big tasks down to into doable pieces. If you have a major goal that feels overwhelming to you—slice and dice it. One step at a time and the mountain is climbed—Now, doesn't that feel great?

DEENA PATEL-WINE

I make the most of all that comes and the least of all that goes.

SARA TEASDALE

Never rely on your PDA or your electronic file for addresses, numbers, and e-mail. Just one computer crash or loss of your PDA or cell phone can render you helpless if you lack a paper backup!

SUZANNA HARWELL

Recharge yourself by rearranging your home or office.
Go for simple and streamlined décor and organization and
you will find you have a fresh new attitude, as well.

WENDY JOLENE

I see something that has to be done and I organize it.

ELINOR GUGGENHEIMER

Pay your bills the same day you receive them—don't even
think about it. Not only will you be more organized,
but your credit rating will improve dramatically!

DAPHNE BUNLERT

Two

Chill

GIVE YOURSELF *a* BREAK

You know the feeling too well: you're worn out. The rope you're dangling at the end of is frayed and about to snap. But you can't stop. Your to-do list is longer than the beginnings of that novel you've been working on, and every second that ticks by is gone forever. STOP! You're no good to anyone in this state—your boss, your best friends, your family, and most of all *you*.

In high school I was a bit of an overachiever, wearing myself to the bone to get good grades and participate in every extracurricular activity I could. Overall I enjoyed it, but I remember waking up one morning and my mother telling me I should stay home from school. I wasn't really sick, but I was exhausted. I didn't know what to make of it—most parents would punish their kids for trying to get out of going to school. But her lesson was partly about perspective. If I was sacrificing my health and my sanity for things that were meant to be fulfilling and fun, what was the point? And she knew better than I that some downtime would refresh me and I could hit the ground running the next day doing what I loved.

Naps. Walks. Quiet time. Meditation. Breathing. Day-dreaming. Baths. A good book. Or maybe, best of all, doing nothing. When's the last time you took a step back and really took a moment for yourself? It's about time. Here are a few famous quotes as well as some tried-and-true suggestions from ladies like you and me for taking good care of number one.

Slow Down

If you realize too acutely how valuable time is,
you are too paralyzed to do anything.

KATHARINE BUTLER HATHAWAY

To achieve the impossible dream, try going to sleep.

JOAN KLEMPNER

Like kids, adults need time-outs too, but it's usually to keep
from doing something bad rather than as punishment.

KATHY FREEMAN

A good rest is half the work.

PROVERB

Relaxation is an art that has been made very difficult
to practice by the conditions of modern civilization.

ALANIS MORISSETTE

For fast-acting relief, try slowing down.

LILY TOMLIN

Regardless of your religion, go inside a local church, temple,
or synagogue and sit for a half an hour when there is no service
happening. Simply sit and enjoy the company of your thoughts,
the mellow lighting, and the reflective atmosphere.

PERINE PARKER

If you don't take naps, take one! Take a nap in the middle of the day when you are unusually overwhelmed. Just doing this once, during an "off limits" time, will renew your sense of self and allow you to stay on task the rest of the time!

DONNA OLICKIN

Take a bath early in the morning, before you begin your daily routine. Get up earlier if you have to, and immerse yourself in the tub. You will have a relaxed day.

POLLY PORTER

Interrupt your daily routine on a weekend by doing *nothing;* it brings a fresh perspective.

CAROL WISEMAN

Laugh Out Loud

You grow up the day you have your first real laugh at yourself.

ETHEL BARRYMORE

Housework can't kill you, but why take a chance?

PHYLLIS DILLER

Remember that thing they say about stopping and counting
to ten? It only works if you're sane enough to count.

ALEX PRESTON

I am woman! I am invincible!

I am pooped!

UNKNOWN

Insanity is my only means of relaxation.

UNKNOWN

Read some young adult fiction–a Nancy Drew book or anything by Lemony Snicket. Get yourself out of the busy adult world and remember what it was like to get lost in a book.

EVELYN VANDERMERE

Here is the opposite of your "to-do list" for work! Make an "I want to do this" list. It can be as adventurous as possible, anything you want to accomplish in your life: plant a gorgeous garden, go to Australia and surf, learn to play piano, hang glide. Just by making the list, you are helping your wild wishes come true!

LOTTE WARNER

Learn and Share

Love the moment, and the energy of that moment
will spread beyond all boundaries.

SISTER CORITA KENT

Take up a new hobby you've always been interested in.
Learning a new skill will make you feel productive,
even if that skill is only for your enjoyment.

LAURA BAKER

Don't forget the simple pleasures of your past. Recently I
remembered a favorite present from my childhood, an origami
kit. I bought myself a new kit and was delighted to find that
making these tiny works of art can still focus and clear my mind.

MABLE EVANS

A potluck with friends may be a simple tradition, but it's one of the most fun and even rewarding to uphold.

FLORENCE ALLEN

A change of scenery is often the easiest way to take time away from our everyday lives. Never underestimate the benefits of a simple day trip alone or with friends.

REBECCA GLEESON

Museums are some of the best places to gain a bit of relaxation and perspective. You have to think about something besides your own problems when surrounded by the evidence of so much other reality.

CANDICE LONG

Listen to music you like and cultivate that interest actively—
go to concerts, listen to CD's you have never heard at the store,
and share your taste with friends. Music communicates to us
on many different levels and your favorite music tends
to transport your mind to its favorite place.

KRIS BHAT

Develop your green thumb—even if you only have a couple
of pots on your deck or fire escape. Learn all about plants
online or at the local nursery and add seasonal plants for
spring and fall. Not only will you be creating beauty,
you will be more in tune with nature and the seasons.

AMBER GUETEBIER

Pets are great happiness boosters. The companionship, love, and entertainment a pet provides, for many people, is as significant as any human relationship. Medical researches have even discovered that petting your pets reduces blood pressure!

MICHELLE STRONG

Grab your wild friends and have a clothing swamp. Set aside clothes or accessories you don't wear, gather with friends who've done the same, and begin a fair trade.
Spice up your wardrobe without spending money!

DEE LOGAN

Let It Go

Forget the past and live the present hour.

SARAH KNOWLES BOLTON

The jump is so frightening between where I am and
where I want to be...because of all I may become
I will close my eyes and leap!

MARY ANNE RADMACHER

Worry does not empty tomorrow of its sorrow;
it empties today of its strength.

CORRIE TEN BOOM

You can always find reasons to work. There will always be one more thing to do. But when people don't take time out, they stop being productive. They stop being happy, and that affects the morale of everyone around them.

CARISA BIANCHI

Wrinkles are called worry lines for a reason.

JANICE THOMPSON

Stress is an ignorant state.
It believes that everything is an emergency.
Nothing is that important.

NATALIE GOLDBERG

Tension is who you think you should be.

Relaxation is who you are.

CHINESE PROVERB

If only we'd stop trying to be happy

we'd have a pretty good time.

EDITH WHARTON

Lose track of time—on a weekend, declare it a "no watch"

weekend! Notice how much more relaxed you will be

if you are not always looking at your watch. Ahhhh.

JULIE HENNESSY

Simplify

Life isn't a matter of milestones but of moments.

ROSE FITZGERALD KENNEDY

There is no need to go to India or anywhere else to find peace.
You will find that deep place of silence right in your room,
your garden, or even your bathtub.

ELISABETH KUBLER-ROSS

To sit in the shade on a fine day, and look upon verdure
is the most perfect refreshment.

JANE AUSTEN

The sound of birds stops the noise in my mind.

CARLY SIMON

Sometimes the most important thing in a whole day
is the rest we take between two deep breaths,
or the turning inwards in prayer for five short minutes.

ETTY HILLESUM

Like water which can clearly mirror the sky and the trees only so
long as its surface is undisturbed, the mind can only reflect the
true image of the Self when it is tranquil and wholly relaxed.

INDRA DEVI

If you can attain repose and calm,
believe that you have seized happiness.

JULIE-JEANNE-ELEONORE DE LESPINASSE

Turn off the television and the radio in your car, office, and
home for one full day. Allow yourself to listen to the silence.

VICTORIA MARTUCCI

To instantaneously relax, slowly take four deep
inhales and exhales. Just focus on your breath
and slowly count to three as you breathe.

JEAN MCINTYRE

One way to really relax is with a warm mug of herbal tea—chamomile is one of the most relaxing of all, while peppermint both stimulates and calms. An orange and rose hip tea is good for unwinding and also adds a healthy dose of vitamin C, too!

ANALEYAH NORTH

Working in the garden gives me something beyond the enjoyment of senses. It gives me a profound sense of inner peace.

RUTH STOUT

Create Calm

Taking time for yourself should never be seen as a burden.
Not on you, and not on anyone else.

ELIZABETH FRANKLIN

People tell you to take care of yourself like it's an easy thing.
It's not. It's a very hard thing sometimes, but
there's no shame in making the effort.

FAITH WALKER

Daily walks are one of my best discoveries.
It's just about the only thing I can do for forty-five minutes
without being interrupted.

FREIDA RAMONE

Take some time for yourself every single day. Even if it's just five minutes. Even if you have to lock the door.

CASSIDY SNOW

It may be a cliché, but there often is nothing better than preparing something special to eat.
Not for your family or your friends, just for you.

FRANCINE LOVETT

Designate one day a month as Retreat Day.
Turn off your phones, radio, television, and computer.
Read. Cook yummy food. Sit in silence. Enjoy!

EMILY LOGAN

Take a walk on your lunch hour!

DEBRA POBLETE

Give yourself flowers—and really do it!
The longest lasting blooms are sunflowers, Peruvian lilies,
and dahlias. Most importantly, getting the flowers will
bring the biggest smile to your face.

LILLIAN CRIST

After washing your hair, allow it to dry naturally in the sun.

WENDY HUNTER

Buy yourself a new loofah, a back brush, or a new washcloth
and body wash with lavender essential oil. Use it!

FRAN PETTERSON

Take yourself out to dinner.

STACY LEVINE

Get a life! People who excel have a life outside of work,
which makes them happier, and therefore, more efficient!

PAYTON ROBINSON

Only when one is connected to one's own core is one
connected to others. And, for me, the core,
the inner spring, can be best refound through solitude.

ANNE MORROW LINDBERGH

If you're usually surrounded by people,
spend a day all by yourself and enjoy the solitude—
and the deliciousness—of your own company.

CYNTHIA MacGREGOR

Three

Create Your Style

FASHION SENSE *and* COMMON SENSE

The essence of your style is all you. It sounds obvious, even silly. But how often do we flip through a magazine or look at others on the street and long to have some other woman's wardrobe, body, or charisma? The best make it look effortless, but we know it rarely is. The great thing about true style is that it stands on its own, and you don't have to judge or envy anyone else to get it *because it's already yours*. Every outfit you admire, every color that lights up your face, every pair of shoes you flip for—they all reflect you at your best, ready to take on the world.

My best friend claims that whenever she's going through a major transformation—being fired or quitting a job, the end of a relationship, or a move—she buys one thing that seems outlandish for the circumstances. Something she may feel she can't quite afford, but that she absolutely loves and will treasure for a long time. She calls it her I'll-never-[work/be happy/fall in love]-again dress, and considers it a kind of reverse-psychology good luck charm. The thinking goes that if she's all washed up, at least she has this one, last, beautiful thing to remember as she wallows in her misery. Of course, she's not one to wallow. And I think the true purpose is to force herself back into the game by embracing beauty in her own way and on her own terms. It cheers her right up to tote around a new bag or get complements on an inspired new 'do. And let me tell you it works for her... she's never been down in the dumps for long (and even if she was she sure wouldn't look it).

After conducting an informal poll of the most stylish women I know, I've put together the 1-2-3 rule. (And of course, the best of the best know how to outdo themselves by breaking every rule.)

1. Simplicity is the key—especially on a budget. Clean lines, strong colors, no fuss.

2. Always feel comfortable in your clothes—if you love the way it looks on the hanger but feel funny every time you put it on, it goes right into the clothes swap pile.

3. Quality over quantity—for the price of a lot of cheap stuff that wears out in one season, buy one great thing you'll have forever.

Express Your Inner Beauty

I think your whole life shows in your face
and you should be proud of that.

LAUREN BACALL

Style may be on the surface,
but you can be deep and still have some.

CLARISSA GOUGH

Looking for a new sense of style? Try a new sense of self first.
It's cheaper, and you won't have to get rid of the impulse buys.

RHONDA BRADFORD

Kindness is always fashionable.

AMELIA BARR

Fashion is not something that exists in dresses only.
Fashion is in the sky, in the street, fashion has to do
with ideas, the way we live, what is happening.

COCO CHANEL

Fashion can be bought. Style one must possess.

EDNA WOOLMAN CHASE

Beauty is how you feel inside, and it reflects in your eyes.

It is not something physical.

SOPHIA LOREN

Fashions are always changing but
our friendships will never go out of style.

DOLLY WRIGHT

Style is based on who you are.

ISABELLA ROSSELLINI

Zest is the secret of all beauty.

There is no beauty that is attractive without zest.

CHRISTIAN DIOR

Of all the things you wear,

your expression is the most important.

JANET LANE

How many cares one loses when one decides

not to be something but to be someone.

COCO CHANEL

There is no cosmetic for beauty like happiness.

MARIA MITCHELL

Show Your Sass

If the shoe fits, it's too expensive.

ADRIENNE GUSOFF

If high heels were so wonderful,

men would be wearing them.

SUE GRAFTON

I base my fashion taste on what doesn't itch.

GILDA RADNER

We are entitled to wear cowboy boots to our own revolution.

NAOMI WOLF

Some women hold up dresses that are so ugly and they always say the same thing: 'This looks much better on.' On what? On fire?

RITA RUDNER

The only rule is don't be boring.... Life is too short to blend in.

PARIS HILTON

Give a girl the correct footwear and she can conquer the world.

BETTE MIDLER

I'm not offended by all the dumb blonde jokes because I know I'm not dumb. I also know I'm not blonde.

DOLLY PARTON

Dear, NEVER forget one little point:
It's MY business. You just work here.

ELIZABETH ARDEN (IN A NOTE TO HER HUSBAND)

I'm a big woman. I need big hair.

ARETHA FRANKLIN

I wouldn't say I invented tacky, but I definitely
brought it to its present high popularity.

BETTE MIDLER

Shop 'Til You Drop, Pamper 'Til You're Pooped

I would rather shop than eat!

WALLIS SIMPSON

I feel sexy when I get out of the tub—your skin is fresh and
you've put up your hair without looking.

SHANIA TWAIN

She had the loaded handbag of someone who camps
out and seldom goes home, or who imagines life
must be full of emergencies.

MAVIS GALLANT

I love color and I love to dress like a woman.

LISA GUERRERO

I don't go out without makeup. I'm a woman, you know.

SHAKIRA

There are no ugly women, only lazy ones.

HELENA RUBINSTEIN

I will buy any creme, cosmetic, or elixir
from a woman with a European accent.

ERMA BOMBECK

Going hungry never bothered me—it was having no clothes!

CHER

Every best-dressed woman keeps some of her gowns
for years. She's learned that fashion-wisdom is compounded
of knowledge, taste, confidence, and poise.

LORETTA YOUNG

You'd be surprised how much it costs to look this cheap.

DOLLY PARTON

The only thing that separates us from the animals
is our ability to accessorize.

OLYMPIA DUKAKIS

Paint your nails in two tones—next time you get a French manicure, ask for lime green and pink, or red and gold, or black with orange tips! Get creative!

OLIVIA LAMONDE

For your next office holiday party, or power-lunch, go vintage! Many higher-end vintage clothing stores sell dresses, suits, and blouses in like-new condition at a fraction of the cost of new designer clothing. These items are usually high quality and add flair to your wardrobe. Vintage clothing creates a classic and unique look.

AMBER RAE

Use your favorite lotion in your hair!
It tames the frizzies and scents your hair beautifully!

MICHELLE STRONG

A purse with panache is a great way to update your wardrobe.
Invest in four (practical) purses you absolutely love and
alternate them on a regular basis. For a quick change of purses,
keep your wallet, cell phone, keys and favorite lipstick in a
small makeup bag that can be transferred at the drop of hat!

EDIE RAVINE

I always say shopping is cheaper than a psychiatrist.

TAMMY FAYE BAKER

Jewelry is a quick and great way to add some pizzazz to your outfit—try sporting your favorite earrings and a dazzling necklace. Once a year, treat yourself and get all your jewelry professionally cleaned—your gems will sparkle like new!

EDIE RAVINE

I take Him shopping with me.
I say, "Okay, Jesus, help me find a bargain."

TAMMY FAYE BAKER

Forget diamonds, a girl's best friend is the perfect-fitting dress!

AMANDA FORD

Buy a collection of essential oil, and make your own fragrances and blends. Start with the basics like lavender, orange, and mint, and expand as you experiment. You can customize your sheets and laundry soap with your new scent. You can even scent your household cleaner by adding a few drops of lavender oil! Create your own signature scent!

RHIANNON MAHONEY

Owning Yourself

Nothing makes a woman more beautiful
than the belief that she is beautiful.

SOPHIA LOREN

We have to have faith in ourselves. I have never met a woman
who, deep down in her core, really believes she has great legs.
And if she suspects that she might have great legs, then she's
convinced that she has a shrill voice and no neck.

CYNTHIA HEIMEL

Fashion trends may not last forever, but the photos will.

ALICE TURNER

Even the most beautiful couture looks shabby
if you can't hold your head high and strike a good pose.

SANDRA COOR

I represent more the healthy, happy, curvy, strong woman.
And that sounds much healthier to me than being
80 pounds and skinny as a bean.

HEIDI KLUM

Toughness doesn't have to come in a pinstripe suit.

DIANNE FEINSTEIN

Get really dressed up for work one day for no other
reason than just "putting your best foot forward,"
your best earrings, a stunning suit or pretty dress and,
obviously, your favorite dressy shoes.

NINA LESOWITZ

We've come a long way. Power dressing now is designed
to let the woman inside us come through.

DONNA KARAN

While clothes may not make the woman, they certainly
have a strong effect on her self-confidence—
which, I believe, does make the woman.

MARY KAY ASH

Vamp It Up

Being a sex symbol has to do with an attitude, not looks.
Most men think it's looks, most women know otherwise.

KATHLEEN TURNER

A woman is no older than she looks.

UNKNOWN

It's no secret that I love a powerful yet slightly fragile
woman such as Garbo, Lillian Gish, Bette Davis...
that's where I get my inspirations from.

SIOBHAN FAHEY

Glamour is what I sell; it's my stock in trade.

MARLENE DIETRICH

There are various orders of beauty, causing men
to make fools of themselves in various styles.

GEORGE ELIOT

Wear red! It is flattering on everyone and
a great alternative to black.

AMBER GUETEBIER

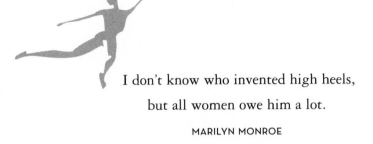

I don't know who invented high heels,
but all women owe him a lot.

MARILYN MONROE

Sex appeal is fifty percent what you've got and
fifty percent what people think you've got.

SOPHIA LOREN

Scratch most feminists and underneath there is a woman
who longs to be a sex object. The difference is
that is not all she wants to be.

BETTY ROLLIN

Brainy Is Beautiful

Any girl can be glamorous.
All you have to do is stand still and look stupid.

HEDY LAMARR

You don't have to signal a social conscience by looking like a frump. Lace knickers won't hasten the holocaust...and a mild interest in the length of hemlines doesn't necessarily disqualify you from reading *Das Kapital* and agreeing with every word.

ELIZABETH BIBESCO

You get out of fashion what you put into it.

LORETTA YOUNG

I'm not interested in age.

People who tell me their age are silly.

You're as old as you feel.

ELIZABETH ARDEN

I'm not obsessed by how I look or with being reed thin, but I
do think that as a woman in my 50s, I have forty years ahead.
Looking after yourself goes hand in hand with looking good.

LINDA EVANS

If truth is beauty, how come no one has
her hair done in a library?

LILY TOMLIN

Don't buy clothes at the last minute, and try to decide
what you are going to wear to an important meeting or date
the night in advance. If possible, try the outfit on a few nights
before the event and wear it around your apartment
to make sure you are comfortable.

EDIE RAVINE

Elegance is refusal.

COCO CHANEL

I began wearing hats as a young lawyer because it helped me
to establish my professional identity. Before that, whenever
I was at a meeting, someone would ask me to get the coffee–
they assumed I was a secretary.

BELLA ABZUG

Four

Gather Your Group

FRIENDS, MENTORS, *and* MOTIVATORS

We need friends. What would life be without them? Lonely, for one. What does friendship mean? Everything cheesy applies. Friends touch our hearts, enrich our lives, bolster our hopes, and forgive our ugly moments. They offer an outside perspective. They know us better than we know ourselves. True friends give sound advice and tell us the truth, even when it hurts. They listen to our woes and our joys, and stand by us when no one else will.

The girl you met on the first day of the second grade. Your mentor at work. The great aunt who swoops into town to take you to a fancy lunch just when you need it most. Friends who share passions or just live down the street. Through friends we are connected by degrees to every other human being on the planet, so friendship really does bind the world together.

Even better, friends are free of charge. There are no legal ties to friendship, no contracts, usually not even a blood relation (though being friends with your mom, sisters, or cousins has its own rewards). They are the people we choose to bond with—and they become our second family. Sometimes they're a way more sane and likable family than the one we're born into.

What about the dreaded fight with your best friend? It leaves you heartsick, and if you can't patch it up you'll feel the ache for a long time to come. Take my advice and do what you can to make it better. Life's too short to live with regrets, and way too short to live without good friends. When I look back on fights with friends, I cringe at my own silly pride.

The only thing better than having a friend is *being* a friend. With friendship comes responsibility—the challenge to look outside ourselves and invest in someone else's happiness. The greatest reward of friendship—helping your friends become their best in every way.

The Wonder of Friends

My true friends have always given me that
supreme proof of devotion, a spontaneous
aversion for the man I loved.

COLETTE

Time spent with friends is healing because
we don't perceive it as time. We just are.

GRACE MORTON

Trouble is like a sieve through which
we sift our acquaintances. Those too big
to pass through are our friends.

ARLENE FRANCIS

To be rich in friends is to be poor in nothing.

LILIAN WHITING

Each friend represents a world in us,
a world possibly not born until they arrive, and it is
only by this meeting that a new world is born.

ANAÏS NIN

A friend is someone who knows all about you
and loves you anyway!

LESLIE ROSSMAN

Though friendship is not quick to burn, it is explosive stuff.

MAY SARTON

Walking with a friend in the dark

is better than walking alone in the light.

HELEN KELLER

The friend who holds your hand and says the wrong thing is

made of dearer stuff than the one who stays away.

BARBARA KINGSOLVER

Happiness is the comfortable companionship of friends.

PAM BROWN

Animals are such agreeable friends,

they ask no questions, they pass no criticisms.

GEORGE ELIOT

What's really important in life—friends, friends, friends.

FANNIE FLAGG

A friend is someone who reaches for your hand
but touches your heart.

KATHLEEN FROVE

Friends are like angels following you through life.

MARY ELLEN

My friends are my estate.

EMILY DICKINSON

Never doubt that a small group of dedicated people can make a difference. Indeed it is the only thing that ever has.

MARGARET MEAD

Life's truest happiness is found in friendships
we make along the way.

LAUREN RUIZ

A friend is someone who knows the song
in your heart, and can sing it back to you
when you have forgotten the words.

DONNA ROBERTS

What Would We Do Without Them?

Loneliness is the most terrible poverty.

MOTHER TERESA

The only true disability would be to go
through life without friendship.

LAURA FORTH

It seems to me that trying to live without friends is like milking
a bear to get cream for your morning coffee. It is a whole lot
of trouble, and then not worth much after you get it.

ZORA NEALE HURSTON

A friend is like a four-leaf clover, hard to find but lucky to have.

SAMANTHA ROSALES

Care and Feeding

A friendship can weather most things and thrive in thin soil; but
it needs a little mulch of letters and phone calls and small, silly
presents every so often—just to save it from drying out completely.

PAM BROWN

Plant a seed of friendship—reap a bouquet of happiness.

LOIS L. KAUFMAN

There may not be a recipe for friendship,
but that doesn't mean there are no rules.

BLANCHE HARDING

They call it "making friends" for a reason.
It takes effort, and the right ingredients.

SANDRA GARRETT

A new friendship is like an unripened fruit—
it may become either an orange or a lemon.

EMMA STACEY

If you judge people, you have no time to love them.

MOTHER TERESA

Silences make the real conversations between friends.
Not the saying but the never needing to say is what counts.

MARAGRET LEE RUNBECK

It takes a lot of courage to show your dreams to someone else.

ERMA BOMBECK

The sharing of joy, whether physical, emotional, psychic, or
intellectual, forms a bridge between the sharers which can be
the basis for understanding much of what is not shared
between them, and lessens the threat of their difference.

AUDRE LORDE

The only thing to do is to hug
one's friends tight and do one's job.

EDITH WHARTON

For women, talk is the glue that holds relationships together;
it creates connections between people and a sense of community.

DEBORAH FARMER

Count your joys instead of your woes/
Count your friends instead of your foes.

IRISH PROVERB

Strangers are just friends waiting to happen!

WENDY WENTWORTH

Make new friends and keep the old,
one is silver and the other is gold.

GIRL SCOUT MOTTO

We are each other's magnitude and bond.

GWENDOLYN BROOKS

"Stay" is a charming word in a friend's vocabulary.

LOUISA MAY ALCOTT

Connection

Friendship is the golden ribbon that ties the world together.

KRISTINA KENTIGLAN

I am treating you as my friend, asking you share my present minuses in the hope I can ask you to share my future pluses.

KATHERINE MANSFIELD

Two may talk together under the same roof for many years, yet never really meet; and two others at first speech are old friends.

MARY CATHERWOOD

Though our communication wanes at times of absence,
I'm aware of a strength that emanates in the background.

CLAUDETTE RENNER

In loneliness, in sickness, in confusion—the mere knowledge
of friendship makes it possible to endure, even if the
friend is powerless to help. It is enough that they exist.

PAM BROWN

Ah, how good it feels...the hand of an old friend.

MARY ENGLEBRIGHT

I don't want to lose this happy space where I have
found someone who is smart and easy and doesn't
bother to check her diary when we arrange to meet.

JEANETTE WINTERSON

There is magic in long-distance friendships.
They let you relate to other human beings in a way that goes
beyond being physically together and is often more profound.

DIANA CORTES

There is no distance too great between friends,
for love gives wings to the heart.

ELIZABETH E. KOEHLER

Some people go to priests; others to poetry; I to my friends.

VIRGINIA WOOLF

Giving

You never lose by loving. You always lose by holding back.

BARBARA DE ANGELIS

If we would build on a sure foundation in friendship,
we must love friends for their sake rather than our own.

CHARLOTTE BRONTË

I don't get women who pick fights with their friends.
It's not like you get to kiss and make up afterwards.
Play those games with your lover if you have to,
but don't toy with a good friendship.

MARCIA BOND

We all need friends with whom we can speak of our deepest concerns, and who do not fear to speak the truth in love to us.

MARGRET GUENTHER

The finest kind of friendship is between two people who expect a great deal of each other, but never ask it.

SYLVIA BREMER

Constant use will not wear ragged the fabric of friendship.

DOROTHY PARKER

The best time to make friends is before you need them.

ETHEL BARRYMORE

It's important to our friends to believe that we are unreservedly frank with them, and important to the friendship that we are not.

MIGNON McLAUGHLIN

Send a thank you note to a good friend, a relative, or coworker "just because" and let them know what you appreciate about them. This "attitude of gratitude" will take you far in your life and will come back to you many times over.

MARY JANE RYAN

A real friend is one who walks in when the rest of the world walks out.

BETH BACHTOLD

Friendship with oneself is all important because without it
one cannot be friends with anybody else in the world.

ELEANOR ROOSEVELT

I've always believed that one woman's success
can only help another woman's success.

GLORIA VANDERBILT

We cherish our friends not for their ability to amuse us,
but for ours to amuse them.

EVELYN WAUGH

A good friend brings out the best in everybody!

MIMI COOKE

Growing

The most beautiful discovery that true friends can make
is that you can grow separately without growing apart.

ELIZABETH FOLEY

All you'll get from strangers is surface pleasantry or indifference.
Only someone who loves you will criticize you.

JUDITH CRIST

Four be the things I am wiser to know:
Idleness, sorrow, a friend, and a foe.

DOROTHY PARKER

No person is your friend who demands your silence,

or denies your right to grow.

ALICE WALKER

Parents start you off on life but friends get you through it.

DEE CHOU

I can trust my friends.

These people force me to examine, encourage me to grow.

CHER

It is the friends you call up at 4AM that matter.

MARLENE DIETRICH

Five

Indulge Yourself

LITTLE REWARDS LEAD to
BIG ACCOMPLISHMENTS

This is going to sound silly, but bear with me. Sometimes I like to think of myself as an animal. Not in some weird role-playing and getting dressed up in costumes with fur and tails kind of way, just like this. I watch my cat spend a good hour hard at play, going after balls of fluff or bits of string with absolute concentration and zeal. And then when she's done, it all falls away. She gives herself a nice bath and curls up for a nap, completely satisfied with her morning.

We live more hectic lives than the average house pet, sure, but maybe there's something to learn from them. They live in the moment, they don't procrastinate, and they don't get neurotic about things beyond their control. They have an amazing ability to focus on the task at hand, and when it's done to let it go and really enjoy their downtime. Maybe I can appeal to my own animal instincts and try to do one thing at a time with all my mental and physical prowess. And then give myself little rewards. Hey, maybe I can even train myself if I promise I get a break with tea and cookies after I fold all that laundry.

Soaking your feet, having a facial, treating yourself to dinner. Or even going beyond the mundane to splurge on a real vacation. Vacations are really important. My godmother taught me to believe that time changes when you go away. A weekend on the beach can erase a month of city tension. And you can learn new things, work through problems, and strengthen relationships at turbo speeds in the parallel vacation universe. Go on, give it a try. Make a commitment to pamper yourself a little on the way to realizing your dreams. Your inner feline will thank you.

You Deserve It

I have an everyday religion that works for me.
Love yourself first, and everything else falls into line.

LUCILLE BALL

To be a saint does not exclude fine dresses nor a beautiful house.

KATHERINE TYNAN HINKSON

Chocolate has iron in it. Surely that's why I like it so much.

ERIN YOUNG

Birds sing after a storm; why shouldn't people feel as free
to delight in whatever remains to them?

ROSE FITZGERALD KENNEDY

As women, we are taught to fear our own desires much more than men. Anything we want, we are told, should be considered suspect.... While it is wise to carefully examine what we want and what we need, wanting in itself should not be so feared.

ALANA PRICE

If you always do what interests you,
then at least one person is pleased.

KATHARINE HEPBURN

I have low self-esteem, but I express it the healthy way...
by eating a box of Double-Stuff Oreos.

MIRANDA (CYNTHIA NIXON), *SEX AND THE CITY*

Money earned with pains should be spent on pleasure.

CHINESE PROVERB

Pleasure that isn't paid for is as insipid as
everything else that's free.

ANITA LOOS

It is in his pleasure that a man really lives; it is from
his leisure that he constructs the true fabric of self.

AGNES REPPLIER

Without leaps of imagination, or dreaming,
we lose the excitement of possibilities.
Dreaming, after all, is a form of planning.

GLORIA STEINEM

Don't Wait

Life is uncertain. Eat dessert first.

ERNESTINE ULMER

Our best gifts to ourselves may be few,
but that doesn't mean they have to be far between.

DELILAH CARR

Seize the moment. Remember all those women
on the 'Titanic' who waved off the dessert cart.

ERMA BOMBECK

You have to treat yourself every once in a while,
get to the fun stuff!

HEIDI KLUM

The essence of pleasure is spontaneity.

GERMAINE GREER

While many fantasies are best left to the realm of the
imagination, some must be fulfilled if we are
to be healthy, growing individuals.

AMANDA BENNET

It is only possible to live happily-ever-after
on a day-to-day basis.

MARGARET BANANA

Never let your senses become dulled to your life.
They are your only links to the world around you.

JUSTINE THOREAU

This very moment is a seed from which
the flowers of tomorrow's happiness grow.

MARGARET LINDSEY

I believe in dreams, not just the kind we have at night.
I think that if we hang on to them, they come true.

DANIELLE STEEL

Life is to be lived.

KATHARINE HEPBURN

The Best Things in Life (and some are free!)

I love luxury. And luxury lies not in richness and
ornateness but in the absence of vulgarity.

COCO CHANEL

Food is, delightfully, an area of licensed sensuality,
of physical delight which will, with luck and
enduring taste buds, last our life long.

ANTONIA TILL

No entertainment is so cheap as reading,
nor any pleasure so lasting.

MARY WORTLEY MONTAGU

Fragrance can have a great effect on our well-being, triggering happy memories or unlocking our sensuality. Indulge in some new oils, candles, or perfumes and enjoy the results.

NANCY KLINE

Call your best friend for no other reason than just to catch up— indulge in laughs, a quick catch-up, and the beauty of friendship.

LEIGH STONE

Music melts all the separate parts of our bodies together.

ANAÏS NIN

Over-the-Top Indulgence

It is impossible to overdo luxury.

FRENCH PROVERB

We owe something to extravagance,
for thrift and adventure seldom go hand in hand.

JENNIE JEROME CHURCHILL

We must deprogram ourselves from the belief that all
indulgence is sinful. Only excess is sinful.

YOLANDA BROOKS

Life itself is the proper binge.

JULIA CHILD

Art may be one of humankind's biggest indulgences,
but it's also basic to our survival.

MARYA WHITBECK

Take care of the luxuries and the necessities
will take care of themselves.

DOROTHY PARKER

To be overcome by the fragrance of flowers
is a delectable form of defeat.

BEVERLY NICHOLS

Try This

Eat outdoors. Enjoy an entire dinner service in the backyard,
or even on a small balcony. If you don't have outdoor space,
head for the park. Use real silverware and cloth napkins. Indulge!

BELINDA DECAMP

Go for a walk in the rain.

CYNTHIA MacGREGOR

Make your bedroom a sensuous place for refuge.
Do your work somewhere else in the house, and decorate
with your favorite colors and textures. It should be your
own special, luxurious hideaway.

KATHRYN LAMONT

Those who allow their day to pass by without practicing
generosity and enjoying life's pleasures are like
a blacksmith's bellows: they breathe but do not live.

PROVERB

When I thought I had seen it all, I went for a ride in a
hot air balloon. The perspective renewed my
sense of awe in the world around me!

PATTY HELMS

Treat yourself to the sweet joy of dreaming of
beautiful things, a fabulous job, a fulfilling relationship.

AMANDA FORD

Every time I get a paycheck, I take a few dollars
from it and set them aside for myself. That way, I have
a small fund for when I see that perfect pair of pumps,
without having to pump my credit card.

BETHANY FLEMMING

Live nutty. Just occasionally. Just once in a while and
see what happens. It brightens up your day.

PAT GURITZ

Whip up an easy batch of your own bath salts. Inexpensive
Epsom salts from the pharmacy will do; for a real treat mix them
with sea salt. Toss them into a Ziploc bag and add a few drops
of your favorite essential oil. Shake the baggy until the oil is
distributed throughout, and then draw yourself a hot bath!

FRANCIS L. BAG

Give yourself a scalp massage
for the next time you wash your hair.

DOLLY WHITTIER

Paint a room in your house or apartment a color
you love—fiery red, bright blue, or lavishing lavender
and enjoy the new ambiance.

LEIGH STONE

Give yourself a break from cooking tonight; instead,
have dinner delivered and enjoy your additional free time.

JENNIFER LEWIS

Far away there in the sunshine are my highest aspirations.
I may not reach them, but I can look up and see their beauty,
believe in them, and try to follow where they lead.

LOUISA MAY ALCOTT

Simple Pleasures

I have a simple philosophy: Fill what's empty.
Empty what's full. Scratch where it itches.

ALICE ROOSEVELT LONGWORTH

It's an indulgence to sit in a room and discuss
your beliefs as if they were a juicy piece of gossip.

LILLIAN HELLMAN

Life in the country teaches one that the really stimulating
things are the quiet, natural things.... The scent of grass
is more luxurious than the most expensive perfume.

BEVERLEY NICHOLS

Real luxury is time and opportunity to read for pleasure.

JANE BRODY

To me a lush carpet of pine needles or spongy grass
is more welcome than the most luxurious Persian rug.

HELEN KELLER

Start a garden and plant it with only your favorite
seasonal flowers. Grow your own special outdoor retreat,
even if it's only a window box.

CYNTHIA KINGSTON

What do I want to take home from my summer vacation? Time.
The wonderful luxury of being at rest. The days when you
shut down ... and let life simply wander.

ELLEN GOODMAN

Buying is a profound pleasure.

SIMONE DE BEAUVOIR

If one could be friendly with women, what
a pleasure–the relationship so secret and private
compared with relations with men.

VIRGINIA WOOLF

Museums and art stores are also sources of pleasure and inspiration…it is true that I derive genuine pleasure from touch.

HELEN KELLER

God made all pleasures innocent.

CAROLINE NORTON

six

Live Well

LIVING YOUR LIFE *to the* HILT

What were your dreams when you were a child? Children draw us in because they are open to learning new things every day, they have boundless energy, and they appreciate beauty in a way many of us have forgotten how to do. My mother still gets tears in her eyes when she remembers my son, at six months old, seeing his first spring. He was looking up at a tree in full flower and his eyes got very wide, and he started crooning up to the tree's branches, singing out a little baby celebration of life.

We're all striving to make the most of what we've got; we all want better lives. But sometimes this desire contorts, and we start to think that if only we had more money, or different circumstances, or just a little greener grass that our lives would be perfect. Well, I am here to attest that perfect is boring—and life is anything but boring. And while more and better stuff might be fun for a while, the real fun starts when we embrace the intangibles. The ingredients of a well-lived life are yours for the choosing: openness, strength, courage, dignity, responsibility, passion, positivity, energy, beauty, and whatever else you fancy.

It's time to take control of your destiny. Time to merge your inner child's enthusiasm with your adult experience. Believe you can live beyond your wildest dreams, voice your desires and act on them, and reap the benefits of a life lived to the hilt!

Uncover Your Soul's Purpose

A bird doesn't sing because it has an answer,
it sings because it has a song.

MAYA ANGELOU

The most important thing you will ever do is become
who you were meant to be. Blossom into yourself.

LISA HAMMOND

Invest in the human soul. Who knows,
it might be a diamond in the rough.

MARY McLEOD BETHUNE

Life is what we make it, always has been, always will be.

GRANDMA MOSES

Don't be afraid your life will end;
be afraid that it will never begin.

GRACE HANSEN

You don't get to choose how you're going to die, or when.
You can only decide how you're going to live now.

JOAN BAEZ

I have always had a dread of becoming a passenger in life.

MARGARET II, QUEEN OF DENMARK

126

In great moments life seems neither right nor wrong,
but something greater: it seems inevitable.

MARGARET SHERWOOD

You are all you will ever have for certain.

JUNE HAVOC

Finding your passion is about connecting the dots
between your head and your heart.

MARIA MARSALA

People are like stained glass windows. They sparkle and shine
when the sun is out, but when the darkness sets in, their true
beauty is revealed only if there is light from within.

ELIZABETH KUBLER-ROSS

I have learned not to worry about love;
but to honor its coming with all my heart.

ALICE WALKER

No trumpets sound when the important decisions
of our live are made. Destiny is made known silently.

AGNES DE MILLE

Some women go through life turning on lamps in the evening.
Others are themselves a light.

HELEN PERKES

The Ingredients of a Wonderful Life

The kind of beauty I want most is the hard-to-get kind
that comes from within: strength, courage, dignity.

RUBY DEE

Life is a mystery as deep as ever death can be.

MARY MAPES DODGE

Eating is not merely a material pleasure. Eating well gives a
spectacular joy to life and contributes immensely to good will
and happy companionship. It is of great importance to the morale.

ELSA SCHIAPARELLI

Good communication is just as stimulating
as black coffee, and just as hard to sleep after.

ANNE MORROW LINDBERGH

The point is not to pay back kindness but to pass it on.

JULIA ALVAREZ

The things we truly love stay with us always,
locked in our hearts as long as life remains.

JOSEPHINE BAKER

The only thing that makes life possible is permanent,
intolerable uncertainty; not knowing what comes next.

URSULA K. LE GUIN

I'm not happy, I'm cheerful. There's a difference.
A happy woman has no cares at all. A cheerful woman
has cares but has learned how to deal with them.

BEVERLY SILLS

The universe is made of stories, not of atoms.

MURIEL RUKEYSER

No one has a right to consume happiness without producing it.

HELEN KELLER

Desire, ask, believe, receive.

STELLA TERRILL MANN

Live as if you like yourself, and it may happen.

MARGE PIERCY

Choice is all we have. Choice is all we need.

KAREN CASEY

Learn to trust your own judgment, learn inner
independence, learn to trust that time will sort
good from bad—including your own bad.

DORIS LESSING

The cure for boredom is curiosity.

There is no cure for curiosity.

ELLEN PARR

Without an open-minded mind,

you can never be a great success.

MARTHA STEWART

Grace, growth, and gratitude: these are my highest aspirations.

GLORIA ARLISS

"Yes" is contagious on a subliminal level.
It affects everything you do.

SARK

Happily, love is a pleasant emotion and
thrives as well in stables as in palaces.

DIANE ACKERMAN

Life is better than death, I believe, if only because
it is less boring, and because it has fresh peaches in it.

ALICE WALKER

134

Count on Your Own Character

Don't compromise yourself. You are all you've got.

JANIS JOPLIN

Civilization is a method of living and an
attitude of equal respect for all people.

JANE ADDAMS

As long as you keep a person down, some part of you
has to be down there to hold him down, so it means
you cannot soar as you otherwise might.

MARIAN ANDERSON

I would rather die a meaningful death
than to live a meaningless life.

CORAZON AQUINO

Character builds slowly, but it can be
torn down with incredible swiftness.

FAITH BALDWIN

You can stand tall without standing on someone.
You can be a victor without having victims.

HARRIET WOODS

We cannot afford not to fight for growth and understanding, even when it is painful, as it is bound to be.

MAY SARTON

Self-respect cannot be hunted.... It comes to us when we are alone, in quiet moments, in quiet places, when we suddenly realize that, knowing the good, we have done it; knowing the beautiful, we have served it; knowing the truth, we have spoken it.

WHITNEY GRISWOLD

If you can't change your fate, change your attitude.

AMY TAN

The willingness to accept responsibility for one's own life is the source from which self-respect springs.

JOAN DIDION

My recipe for life is not being afraid of myself, afraid of what I think, or of my opinions.

EARTHA KITT

Live in Your Prime All the Time

The hardest years in life are those between ten and seventy.

HELEN HAYES

The history of all times, and of today especially, teaches that...
women will be forgotten if they forget to think about themselves.

LOUISE OTTO

Strive for Five—try to learn five new words a week; it keeps
your brain active and helps your memory skills. Also, a wild
woman with a very large vocabulary is a potent combination.

AUTUMN STEPHENS

So much has been said and sung of beautiful young girls,
why doesn't somebody wake up to the beauty of old women?

HARRIET BEECHER STOWE

One's prime is elusive. You little girls, when you grow up,
must be on the alert to recognize your prime at
whatever time of your life it may occur.

MURIEL SPARK

The wisdom acquired with the passage of time
is a useless gift unless you share it.

ESTHER WILLIAMS

I hope when this life is over, people will say of me, "She lived, she laughed, she loved with all that she was." Consider what you want people to remember of you and live accordingly.

BARB ROGERS

I learned a woman is never an old woman.

JONI MITCHELL

If we had no winter, the spring would not be so pleasant;
if we did not sometimes taste of adversity,
prosperity would not be so welcome.

ANNE BRADSTREET

Age is something that doesn't matter, unless you are a cheese.

BILLIE BURKE

What a wonderful life I've had! I only wish I'd realized it sooner.

COLETTE

I am beautiful as I am. I am the shape that was gifted.
My breasts are no longer perky and upright like when I was a
teenager. My hips are wider than that of a fashion model's.
For this I am glad, for these are the signs of a life lived.

CINDY OLSEN

What is amazing for a woman of my age is that I change
as the world is changing—and changing very, very fast.
I don't think my mother had that opportunity to change.

JEANNE MOREAU

The secret of staying young is to live honestly,
eat slowly, and lie about your age.

LUCILLE BALL

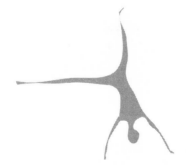

Grow to Learn, Learn to Grow

I don't want to get to the end of my life and find that I lived
just the length of it. I want to have lived the width of it as well.

DIANE ACKERMAN

A really strong woman accepts the war
she went through and is ennobled by her scars.

CARLY SIMON

Fortunately, psychoanalysis is not the only way to resolve
inner conflicts. Life itself remains a very effective therapist.

KAREN HORNEY

You must learn day by day, year by year, to broaden your horizon. The more things you love, the more you are interested in, the more you enjoy, the more you are indignant about, the more you have left when anything happens.

ETHEL BARRYMORE

People don't live nowadays: they get about ten percent out of life.

ISADORA DUNCAN

Happiness must be cultivated. It is like character. It is not a thing to be safely let alone for a moment, or it will run to weeds.

ELIZABETH STUART PHELPS

One is not born a woman, one becomes one.

SIMONE DE BEAUVOIR

You need only claim the events of your life to make yourself yours. When you truly possess all that you have been and done, which may take some time, you are fierce with reality.

FLORIDA SCOTT MAXWELL

If we don't change, we don't grow. If we don't grow, we are not really living. Growth demands a temporary surrender of security.

GAIL SHEEHY

Adventure is worthwhile in itself.

AMELIA EARHART

At the moment you are most in awe of all there is
about life that you don't understand, you are closer
to understanding it all than at any other time.

JANE WAGNER

Learn to get in touch with the silence within yourself and
know that everything has a purpose. There are no mistakes,
no coincidences, all events are blessings given to us to learn from.

ELIZABETH KUBLER-ROSS

Mistakes are part of the dues one pays for a full life.

SOPHIA LOREN

Random acts of kindness—simple acts of generosity, are not only nice for other people but they actually are healthy for you physically as well as spiritually. It reduces levels of stress hormones. So, go ahead and make yourself and others happy today!

MARY RUSKIN

Life engenders life. Energy creates energy.
It is by spending oneself that one becomes rich.

SARAH BERNHARDT

Seven

Be Bold

HOW *to* MAKE YOUR IDEAS COUNT

Your mother always told you to be careful. Look both ways before crossing the street, don't lose track of your wallet and keys, hold the handrail on those icy steps. And I'm with her all the way in terms of that kind of stuff. But being careful can be taken too far, you know. What happens if we never risk looking silly, or don't challenge ourselves by pushing our intellect to the limit, or refuse to take the chance of falling head over heels in love? Well, we lose. Big time.

I have lived my whole life terrified of failure. Even as a small child, if I couldn't do something right on the first try, I gave up. Somewhere along the line in school I stopped learning for fun and started trying to prove how smart I was. Now, you know how you can't really make any progress without making mistakes? I've tried never to make mistakes, and when I have I've rarely been able to own up and really take responsibility. Too often I've given up real personal growth in favor of nominal perfection. I'm just starting to realize now how much I've been missing out on a healthy dose of what makes life worth living-risk, irreverence, courage, and growth.

Some people seem to have a knack for it. We say they march to their own drummer; we're wowed by their resilience in the face of criticism and adversity. If you are one of those people, it's time to share your secrets with the rest of us and be a cheerleader for the timid among us. And if you're not one of those people yet, remember that we can all choose to put ourselves on the line as we go after our dreams, and we can always try to use our mistakes as lessons on the road to success. Decide that what you want is more important than your fear of getting it, and there is no stopping you. Nothing ventured, nothing gained. Life's an adventure, so get gaining!

Inner Strength

A sheltered life can be a daring life as well.
For all serious daring starts from within.

EUDORA WELTY

I never realized until lately that women
were supposed to be the inferior sex.

KATHARINE HEPBURN

It's better to be a lion for a day than a sheep all your life.

SISTER ELIZABETH KENNY

Our strength is often composed of the
weakness we're damned if we're going to show.

MIGNON McLAUGHLIN

Men are taught to apologize for their weaknesses,
women for their strengths.

LOIS WYSE

We women talk too much,
nevertheless we only say half of what we know.

NANCY ASTOR

There is a growing strength in women,
but it is in the forehead, not in the forearm.

BEVERLY SILLS

I've been through it all, baby. I'm mother courage.

ELIZABETH TAYLOR

More than anything, I think as our
country matures, we recognize that women deserve
to be treated with respect and dignity.

BARBARA BOXER

A woman is like a tea bag—you can't tell how
strong she is until you put her in hot water.

ELEANOR ROOSEVELT

Always be a first-rate version of yourself, instead of
a second-rate version of somebody else.

JUDY GARLAND

Remember no one can make you feel
inferior without your consent.

ELEANOR ROOSEVELT

It's sexy to be competent.

LETTY COTTIN POGREBIN

If you do things well, do them better.
Be daring, be first, be different, be just.

ANITA RODDICK

You were once wild here. Don't let them tame you.

ISADORA DUNCAN

I'm tough, ambitious, and
I know exactly what I want.

MADONNA

I think that women making no apology
for being women is very refreshing.

DREW BARRYMORE

Real power is when you are doing exactly what
you are supposed to be doing the best it can be done.

OPRAH WINFREY

Shaking Things Up

If you think you are too small to be effective,
you have never been in bed with a mosquito.

BETTY REESE

We lift our voices as one;
let all know, we are here, and we intend to stay!

NANCY FREDERICK

Cautious, careful people always casting about to preserve their
reputation or social standards never can bring about reform.
Those who are really in earnest are willing to be anything or
nothing in the world's estimation...and bear the consequences.

SUSAN B. ANTHONY

We've chosen the path to equality, don't let them turn us around.

GERALDINE FERRARO

If particular care and attention is not paid to the ladies, we are determined to foment a rebellion, and will not hold ourselves bound by any laws in which we have no voice or representation.

ABIGAIL ADAMS

Justice is better than chivalry if we cannot have both.

ALICE STONE BLACKWELL

I am in the world to change the world.

MURIEL RUKEYSER

I believe in a lively disrespect for most forms of authority.

RITA MAE BROWN

I prefer liberty to chains of diamonds.

LADY MARY WORTLEY MONTAGU

Women belong in the house. . .and the Senate.

UNKNOWN

What is enough? Enough is when somebody says,
'Get me the best people you can find' and nobody
notices when half of them turn out to be women.

LOUISE RENNE

You can't get swept off your feet if you are sitting down.
Stand up and be noticed!

CLAIRE CAMDEN

Men have always been afraid that women
could get along without them.

MARGARET MEAD

It's been a lot of fun making the revolution.

·BETTY FRIEDAN

I'll not listen to reason. Reason always means
what someone else has got to say.

ELIZABETH GASKELL

Be a Bad Girl in a Good Way

Good girls go to heaven, bad girls go everywhere.

HELEN GURLEY BROWN

Well behaved women rarely make history.

LAUREL THATCHER ULRICH

I do not want people to be agreeable,
as it saves me the trouble of liking them.

JANE AUSTEN

Only good girls keep diaries. Bad girls don't have time.

TALLULAH BANKHEAD

When the sun comes up, I have morals again.

ELAYNE BOOSLER

A woman can look both moral and exciting...

if she also looks as if it was quite a struggle.

EDNA FERBER

Rules are for people who don't know how to get around them.

TORI HARRISON

I have too many fantasies to be a housewife.

I guess I am a fantasy.

MARILYN MONROE

One wonders what would happen in a society in which
there were no rules to break. Doubtless everyone
would quickly die of boredom.

SUSAN HOWITCH

I am not eccentric. It's just that I am more alive than most
people. I am an unpopular electric eel set in a pond of goldfish.

DAME EDITH SITWELL

Women complain about PMS, but I think of it
as the only time of the month that I can be myself.

ROSEANNE BARR

Women are the real architects of society.

HARRIET BEECHER STOWE

I'm extraordinarily patient
provided I get my own way in the end.

MARGARET THATCHER

I've always taken risks, and never worried what
the world might really think of me.

CHER

I can, therefore I am.

SIMONE WEIL

Some say the glass is half empty, some say the glass
is half full, I say, are you going to drink that?

LISA CLAYMEN

If I had to live my life again,
I'd make the same mistakes, only sooner.

TALLULAH BANKHEAD

Until you lose your reputation, you never realize
what a burden it was or what freedom really is.

MARGARET MITCHELL

Facing Challenges

I'm not afraid of storms, for I'm learning to sail my ship.

LOUISA MAY ALCOTT

You can't be brave if you've only
had wonderful things happen to you.

MARY TYLER MOORE

Remember that fear is something learned.
None of us are born afraid.

MARY STANYAN

Whatever women do they must do twice as well as men
to be thought half as good. Luckily, this is not difficult.

CHARLOTTE WHITTON

If you want anything said, ask a man.

If you want something done, ask a woman.

MARGARET THATCHER

The naked truth is always better than the best-dressed lie.

ANN LANDERS

If it's a woman, its caustic; if it's a man, it's authoritative.

BARBARA WALTERS

If Rosa Parks had taken a poll before she sat down
in the bus in Montgomery, she'd still be standing.

MARY FRANCES BERRY

I once complained to my father that I didn't seem to be able to do things the same way other people did. Dad's advice? 'Margo, don't be a sheep. People hate sheep. They eat sheep.'

MARGO KAUFMAN

Speak up for yourself, or you'll end up a rug.

MAE WEST

And the trouble is, if you don't risk anything, you risk more.

ERICA JONG

Unleash Your Desire and Reach for Your Stars

When you have a dream, you've got to grab it and never let it go.

CAROL BURNETT

I think the key is for women not to set any limits.

MARTINA NAVRATILOVA

There are no dangerous thoughts; thinking itself is dangerous.

HANNAH ARENDT

Truth is always exciting. Speak it, then; life is dull without it.

PEARL S. BUCK

Be bold. If you're going to make an error,
make a doozey, and don't be afraid to hit the ball.

BILLIE JEAN KING

Be bold in what you stand for and careful what you fall for.

RUTH BOORSTIN

To tell a woman everything she may not do
is to tell her what she can do.

SPANISH PROVERB

You may be imperious, but the effect

is always spoiled when you apologize.

KAREN WILLIAMS

Real women don't have flushes, they have power surges.

SANDRA CABOT

When you believe in your dreams you are able to fight for them.

CECILY BARRY

All good fortune is a gift of the gods, and you don't win the

favor of the ancient gods by being good, but by being bold.

ANITA BROOKNER

The thing women have yet to learn is
nobody gives you power. You just take it.

ROSEANNE BARR

If you don't act as if your name
were on the door, it never will.

PATRICIA FRIPP

It's hard to be free, but when it works, it is sure worth it.

JANIS JOPLIN

Bite off more than you can chew, then chew it.

ELLA WILLIAMS

The most effective way to do it, is to do it.

AMELIA EARHART

Life shrinks or expands in proportion to one's courage.

ANAÏS NIN

Eight

Work Smart

LOVING YOUR JOB *and*
BEING THE BEST YOU CAN BE!

In the past few years I've gotten into reading biographies and auto-biographies of people whose lives and work inspire me. I've noticed that even in the case of the "overnight successes," you have to get at least halfway through the book before the hard work starts to pay off in any substantial way. I'm talking chapter after chapter of working for no recognition, no pay, and no glory. Years or even decades of disappointments, detours, and being down in the dumps. But these people struggle through, some even find joy in the adversity. And somewhere in my reading I think, "Right, of course!"

Pay, glory, and recognition are all great, but they aren't real motivators. If that's all you're working toward, you're probably never going to get there. Doing what you love and loving what you do is the real point. Then all that other stuff can be icing on the cake if and when it comes around. And even if you never get the kudos you deserve, you'll hardly notice as you chug along reaping the rewards of a challenging, interesting career.

Dream up a goal, make a plan, and stay present in the moment as you work it out. Evaluate yourself and those around you honestly as you go, and keep the bigger picture in the forefront of your mind. You're going to have to think up new ways to work around obstacles, and you're going to have to battle some drudgery. That might be the hardest part. One way is to keep a reminder of your goals close at hand—a picture, a poem, a sketch—and look at it to help motivate you through the boring stuff. Get your nose to the grindstone, and watch as your worries fall away. Get your hands a little dirty and you're well on your way to being the best you can be.

Work as if It's Fulfilling

Work itself is the reward. If I choose challenging work it will pay me back with interest…. This attempt for excellence is what sustains the most well-lived and satisfying, successful lives.

MERYL STREEP

People think at the end of the day that a man is the only answer [to fulfillment]. Actually a job is better for me.

DIANA, PRINCESS OF WALES

Nothing gratifies one more than to be admired for doing what one likes.

DOROTHY L. SAYERS

I've never been a fan of work as it's usually defined by other
people. But when I learned how to define it for myself,
I realized that it actually can be as fulfilling as I'd always hoped.

BELINDA CASSIDY

Look at a day when you are supremely satisfied at the end.
It's not a day when you lounge around doing nothing;
it's when you've had everything to do, and you've done it.

MARGARET THATCHER

Work won't always make your heart sing.
But when it does, it's one of the best feelings there is.

AMY PORTER

To follow without halt, one aim; there is the secret of success.
And success? What is it? I do not find it in the applause of
the theater; it lies rather in the satisfaction of accomplishment.

ANNA PAVLOVA

Laziness may appear attractive, but work gives satisfaction.

ANNE FRANK

I look back on my life like a good day's work;
it was done and I am satisfied with it.

GRANDMA MOSES

Succeed and Succeed Again

What we really want to do is what we are really meant to do. When we do what we are meant to do, money comes to us, doors open for us, we feel useful, and the work we do feels like play to us.

JULIA CAMERON

You are not in business to be popular.

KIRSTIE ALLEY

The most popular labor-saving device is still money.

PHYLLIS GEORGE

Work is the world's easiest escape from boredom
and the only surefire road to success.

MARABEL MORGAN

The ability to control one's own destiny…
comes from constant hard work and courage.

MAYA ANGELOU

To fulfill a dream, to be allowed to sweat over lonely labor,
to be given a chance to create, is the meat and potatoes of life.
The money is the gravy.

BETTE DAVIS

Measure not the work until the day's out and the labor is done.

ELIZABETH BARRETT BROWNING

Women hold up half the sky.

CHINESE PROVERB

Instead of thinking about where you are,
think about where you want to be. It takes twenty years
of hard work to become an overnight success.

DIANA RANKIN

What I know is, is that if you do work that you love,
and the work fulfills you, the rest will come.

OPRAH WINFREY

Find Your Balance

You cannot be really first-rate at your work

if your work is all you are.

ANNA QUINDLEN

I believe you are your work. Don't trade the stuff of your life,

time, for nothing more than dollars. That's a rotten bargain.

RITA MAE BROWN

Take your work seriously, but never yourself.

MARGOT FONTEYN

Any woman who has a career and a family automatically develops
something in the way of two personalities, like two sides
of a dollar bill, each different in design.... Her problem is
to keep one from draining the life from the other.

IVY BAKER PRIEST

A human being must have occupation if he or she
is not to become a nuisance to the world.

DOROTHY L. SAYERS

Value work. But not any kind of work. Ask yourself,
'Is the work vital, strengthening my own character,
or inspiring others, or helping the world?'

ANNA ROBERTSON BROWN

Work Smart and Stick It Out

Women have to be a lot smarter and brighter and have to work
a lot harder to prepare themselves. They have to watch what
they do and how they behave. It's not a free world yet.

LETITIA BALDRIDGE

The test for whether or not you can hold a job
should not be the arrangement of your chromosomes.

BELLA ABZUG

Nighttime is really the best time to work. All the ideas
are there to be yours because everyone else is asleep.

CATHERINE O'HARA

Hard work need not always be a chore.

At least not outside the house.

JENNIFER CROWLEY

All work done mindfully rounds us out,

helps complete us as persons.

MARSHA SINETAR

When her last child is off to school, we don't want the

talented woman wasting her time in work far below

her capacity. We want her to come out running.

MARY INGRAHAM BUNTING

I am independent! I can live alone and I love to work.

MARY CASSATT

I hate housework. You make the beds, you wash the dishes
and six months later you have to start all over again.

JOAN RIVERS

People have to feel needed. Frequently, we just offer a job and
'perks.' We don't always offer people a purpose. When people
feel there is a purpose and that they're needed, there's
not much else to do except let them do the work.

MAYA ANGELOU

The days you work are the best days.

GEORGIA O'KEEFFE

To work in the world lovingly means that we are defining what
we will be for, rather than reacting to what we are against.

CHRISTINA BALDWIN

Personally, I have nothing against work, particularly when
performed, quietly and unobtrusively, by someone else. I just
don't happen to think it's an appropriate subject for an "ethic."

BARBARA EHRENREICH

If hard work were such a wonderful thing,
surely the rich would have kept it all to themselves.

LANE KIRKLAND

Always be smarter than the people who hire you.

LENA HORNE

Work is something you can count on,
a trusted, lifelong friend who never deserts you.

MARGARET BOURKE-WHITE

Rather than sit around, I'll work.

KELLY LYNCH

I work as often as I want and yet I'm free as a bird.

ETHEL MERMAN

...look and listen hard, do not be discouraged by rejections—
we've all had them many times—and revise your work.

JOYCE CAROL OATES

Attempt the impossible in order to improve your work.

BETTE DAVIS

Aerodynamically the bumblebee shouldn't be able to fly, but the bumblebee doesn't know that so it goes on flying anyway.

MARY KAY ASH

Yesterday I dared to struggle. Today I dare to win.

BERNADETTE DEVLIN

Plan your work for today and every day, then work your plan.

MARGARET THATCHER

There are two kinds of people, those who do the work and those who take credit. Try to be in the first group; there is less competition there.

INDIRA GANDHI

Opportunities are often disguised as hard work,
so most people don't recognize them.

ANN LANDERS

I would rather make mistakes in kindness and compassion
than work miracles in unkindness and hardness.

MOTHER TERESA

Goals are dreams within deadlines.

DIANA SCHARF HUNT

Apply Some Elbow Grease

The biggest sin is sitting on your ass.

FLORYNCE KENNEDY

When it comes to getting things done,
we need fewer architects and more bricklayers.

COLLEEN C. BARRETT

By and large, mothers and housewives are the only workers who
do not have regular time off. They are the great vacationless class.

ANNE MORROW LINDBERGH

Don't feel entitled to anything you didn't sweat and struggle for.

MARIAN WRIGHT EDELMAN

Nobody ever drowned in his own sweat.

ANN LANDERS

Luck? I don't know anything about luck. I've never banked on it,
and I'm afraid of people who do. Luck to me is something else:
hard work—and realizing what is opportunity and what isn't.

LUCILLE BALL

The only thing that ever sat its way to success was a hen.

SARAH BROWN

The sweat of hard work is not to be displayed.
It is much more graceful to appear favored by the gods.

MAXINE HONG KINGSTON

Whatever muscles I have are the product of
my own hard work and nothing else.

EVELYN ASHFORD

Inspiration usually comes during work, rather than before it.

MADELEINE L'ENGLE

Creativity comes from trust. Trust your instincts.

And never hope more than you work.

RITA MAE BROWN

I didn't have to work until I was three.

But after that, I never stopped.

MARTHA RAYE

About the only thing that comes to us without effort is old age.

GLORIA PITZER

Nothing will work unless you do.

MAYA ANGELOU

For the Love of It

Work is either fun or drudgery.
It depends on your attitude. I like fun.

COLLEEN C. BARRETT

Career is too pompous a word. It was a job, and
I have always felt privileged to be paid for what I love doing.

BARBARA STANWYCK

You know you are on the road to success
if you would do your job and not be paid for it.

OPRAH WINFREY

All the things I love is what my business is about.

MARTHA STEWART

To love what you do and feel that it matters—

how could anything be more fun?

KATHERINE GRAHAM

nine

Achieve

WOMEN CAN DO ANYTHING!

Making great strides in the face of adversity. Holding down the fort while dreaming up the next great thing. Hurtling over massive barriers to their success with creative leaps and bounds. Just think: women have been doing all this since the beginning of time, and it doesn't look to be slowing down any time soon. You may cram more into your day and get paid less for it, get fewer big breaks, struggle to make your ideas heard, but you know what? You're up to this challenge.

But wait. In creeps fear; in slithers self-doubt. Are we more susceptible to these, too? Maybe so, because we're in tune with our feelings and those of the people around us. But we have to remember that the flip side of our self-doubt is our ability to empathize—the emotional intelligence that serves us in every relationship we have, from the bedroom to the boardroom. And let's be honest with ourselves. As Marianne Williamson put it so well, "Our deepest fear is not that we are inadequate. Our deepest fear is that we are powerful beyond measure." Know yourself, and don't hold back. Give yourself permission to find the best of you and let it shine without shame or apology. Nobody's going to benefit from your hesitation—you've got too much to get done to keep your talents hidden away so that others are more comfortable around you.

Dare to be powerful. Try it out. All those clichés—roll with the punches, just do it, you'll never know until you try, you can do anything you set your mind to—well, they get stuck in our heads because they're true. So go for it!

Believe In Yourself

To believe in something not yet proved and to underwrite it with our lives: it is the only way we can leave the future open.

LILLIAN SMITH

Only with a steady heart can true excellence be reached.

MOIRA LANDON

I can honestly say that I was never affected by the question of the success of an undertaking. If I felt it was the right thing to do, I was for it regardless of the possible outcome.

GOLDA MEIR

Everyone has talent. What is rare is the courage
to follow talent to the dark place where it leads.

ERICA JONG

It's not so much how busy you are, but why you are busy.
The bee is praised; the mosquito is swatted.

MARIE O'CONNER

Do not follow where the path may lead.
Go instead where there is no path and leave a trail.

MURIEL STRODE

One must fight for a life of action, not reaction.

RITA MAE BROWN

A sobering thought: what if, at this very moment,

I am living up to my full potential?

JANE WAGNER

Women share with men the need for personal success,

even the taste of power, and no longer are we willing

to satisfy those needs through the achievements of surrogates,

whether husbands, children, or merely role models.

ELIZABETH DOLE

Please know that I am quite aware of the hazards.

Women must try to do things as men have tried.

When they fail, their failure must be but a challenge to others.

AMELIA EARHART

A woman can do anything. She can be traditionally
feminine and that's all right; she can work, she can stay
at home; she can be passive; she can be aggressive,
she can be any way she wants with a man.

BARBARA WALTERS

Inaction, contrary for its reputation as being a refuge,
is neither safe nor comfortable.

MADELINE KUHN

Getting ahead in a difficult profession requires avid faith in
yourself. That is why some people with mediocre talent,
but with great inner drive, go much further than
people with vastly superior talent.

SOPHIA LOREN

It is above all by the imagination that
we achieve perception and compassion and hope.

URSULA K. Le GUIN

I have dreamed in my life, dreams that have stayed with me after,
and changed my ideas; they have gone through and through me,
like wine through water, and altered the color of my mind.

EMILY BRONTË

Believe in yourself: across all ages, studies have shown
that a solid believer in one's own abilities increases
life satisfaction by over 40%, and makes us happier
both in our work and home lives.

MEG DESMOND

Overcoming Challenges and Fears

You gain strength, courage and confidence by every experience
in which you really stop to look fear in the face....
You must do the thing you think you cannot do.

ELEANOR ROOSEVELT

You may be disappointed if you fail,
but you are doomed if you don't try.

BEVERLY SILLS

You can do one of two things; just shut up,
which is something I don't find easy, or learn
an awful lot very fast, which is what I tried to do.

JANE FONDA

If we are to achieve a richer culture, rich in contrasting values,
we must recognize the whole gamut of human potentialities,
and so weave a less arbitrary social fabric, one in which
each diverse gift will find a fitting place.

MARGARET MEAD

It irritates me to be told how things have always been done.
I defy the tyranny of precedent. I cannot afford the luxury of a
closed mind. I go for anything that might improve the past.

CLARA BARTON

You can't build a reputation on what you intend to do.

LIZ SMITH

Success will come to you in direct proportion
to the number of times you are willing to risk failure.

PAT GURITZ

Because I am a woman, I must make unusual efforts to succeed.
If I fail, no one will say, 'She doesn't have what it takes.'
They will say, 'Women don't have what it takes.'

CLARE BOOTHE LUCE

I really don't think life is about the I-could-have-beens.
Life is only about the I-tried-to-do. I don't mind the failure
but I can't imagine that I'd forgive myself if I didn't try.

NIKKI GIOVANNI

A champion is afraid of losing. Everyone else is afraid of winning.

BILLIE JEAN KING

You'll never do a whole lot unless you're brave enough to try.

DOLLY PARTON

Risk! Risk anything! Care no more for the opinion of others,

for those voices. Do the hardest thing on earth for you.

Act for yourself. Face the truth.

KATHERINE MANSFIELD

When I dare to be powerful—to use my strength
in the service of my vision—then it becomes less and less
important whether or not I am afraid.

AUDRE LORDE

If you just set out to be liked, you would be
prepared to compromise on anything at any time,
and you would achieve nothing.

MARGARET THATCHER

Sweet Successes

Fearless women go to the top.

BETH BACHTOLD

For what is done or learned by one class of women becomes, by
virtue of their common womanhood, the property of all women.

ELIZABETH BLACKWELL

Not only have women been successful in entering fields
in which men are supposed to have a more natural aptitude,
but they have created entirely new businesses.

LUCRETIA P. HUNTER

Winning may not be everything,
but losing has little to recommend it.

DIANNE FEINSTEIN

The worst part of success is to try to find
someone who is happy for you.

BETTE MIDLER

The women of today are the thoughts of their mothers and
grandmothers, embodied and made alive. They are active,
capable, determined, and bound to win.... Millions of
women dead and gone are speaking through us today.

MATILDA JOSLYN GAGE

Security is not the meaning of my life.
Great opportunities are worth the risk.

SHIRLEY HUFSTEDLER

I don't think any change in the world has been more significant than the change in the status of women.... A woman's world was her home, her family, and perhaps a little community service. Today, a woman's world is as broad as the universe.

BELLE S. SPAFFORD

If I had learned to type,
I never would have made brigadier general.

ELIZABETH P. HOISINGTOM

Don't confuse "things" with success—you are neither
better nor worse for where you live, what you drive,
or the size of your bank account. Remember what really
matters in your life—and it is not "stuff."

MARY JANE RYAN

Getting to the top isn't bad, and it's probably
best done as an afterthought.

ANNE WILSON SCHAEF

Take Little Steps, Make Huge Strides

Success is not a doorway, it's a staircase.

DOTTIE WALTERS

I am only one; but still I am one. I cannot do everything,
but still I can do something. I will not refuse
to do the something I can do.

HELEN KELLER

We must not, in trying to think about how we can make a big
difference, ignore the small daily difference we can make which,
over time, add up to big differences that we often cannot foresee.

MARIAN WRIGHT EDELMAN

Don't wait for your ship to come in, and feel angry and
cheated when it doesn't. Get going with something small.

IRENE KASSORLA

How wonderful it is that nobody needs to wait a
single moment before starting to improve the world.

ANNE FRANK

Do not wait for leaders; do it alone, person to person.

MOTHER TERESA

I'm always moving forward.

DEBBIE ALLEN

I believe the choice to be excellent begins with
aligning your thoughts and words with
the intention to require more from yourself.

OPRAH WINFREY

Strive for excellence, each and every day.

MARION CONDIT

Never Give Up

Just don't give up trying to do what you really
want to do. Where there is love and inspiration,
I don't think you can go wrong.

ELLA FITZGERALD

Always continue the climb. It is possible for you to do whatever
you choose, if you first get to know who you are and are
willing to with a power that is greater than ourselves to do it.

OPRAH WINFREY

Something which we think is impossible now
is not impossible in another decade.

CONSTANCE BAKER MOTLEY

When I stand before God at the end of my life, I would
hope that I would not have a single bit of talent left,
and could say, 'I used everything you gave me.'

ERMA BOMBECK

I never see what has been done;
I only see what remains to be done.

MARIE CURIE

The way I see it, if you want the rainbow,
you gotta put up with the rain.

DOLLY PARTON

Human successes, like human failures, are composed of
one action at a time and achieved by one person at a time.

PATSY H. SAMPSON

I think one's feelings waste themselves in words;
they ought all to be distilled into actions which bring results.

FLORENCE NIGHTINGALE

The only sin is mediocrity.

MARTHA GRAHAM

Perseverance is failing nineteen times
and succeeding the twentieth.

JULIE ANDREWS

Learning is not attained by chance,
it must be sought for with ardor and diligence.

ABIGAIL ADAMS

I'm not going to limit myself because people
won't accept the fact that I can do something else.

DOLLY PARTON

No matter how tough, no matter what kind of outside pressure,
no matter how many bad breaks along the way, I must keep
my sights on the final goal, to win...with more love and passion
than the world has ever witnessed in any performance.

BILLIE JEAN KING

If you don't like something, change it.

If you can't change it, change your attitude.

Don't complain.

MAYA ANGELOU

There's a big difference between seeing an opportunity

and seizing an opportunity.

PAT GURITZ

I didn't get here by dreaming about it or thinking about it—

I got here by doing it. We can do anything we want

to do if we stick with it long enough.

HELEN KELLER

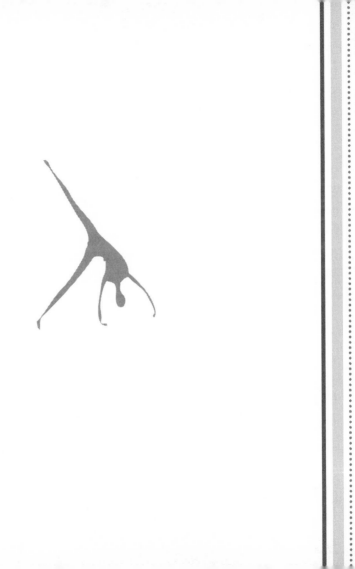

About the Author

Mina Parker is a freelance writer and the mom of an active son, who has learned to run and is starting to talk up a storm. Her other three books for Conari Press are *Half Full* (2006), *Mother Is a Verb* (2007), and *100 Good Wishes for Baby* (2007). She lives in Brooklyn, New York.

To Our Readers

Conari Press, an imprint of Red Wheel/Weiser, publishes books on topics ranging from spirituality, personal growth, and relationships to women's issues, parenting, and social issues. Our mission is to publish quality books that will make a difference in people's lives—how we feel about ourselves and how we relate to one another. We value integrity, compassion, and receptivity, both in the books we publish and in the way we do business.

Our readers are our most important resource, and we value your input, suggestions, and ideas about what you would like to see published. Please feel free to contact us, to request our latest book catalog, or to be added to our mailing list.

Conari Press
An imprint of Red Wheel/Weiser, LLC
500 Third Street, Suite 230
San Francisco, CA 94107
www.redwheelweiser.com